Live the Fullest Of your life
Simple ways to be happy

Dr. Mohsen Khabbari

Copyright © 2021 Mohsen khabbari

All rights reserved. No part of this publication maybe reproduced, distributed or transmitted in any form without the prior written permission of the publisher or author , for permission contact

Foundations of life

Ottawa, Ontario

www.foundationsoflife.ca

ISBN: 9798711771074

To my parents who passed away

Table of Contents

Introduction 5

Chapter one
Financial 9
Focus 9
Spiritual 10
Emotions 11
Diet and Fitness 12
Relationship 13
Family 14
Recreational and Sleep Pattern 14

Chapter two
Financial goals 25
Focus 27
Surroundings 27

Chapter three
Diet and Fitness 29
Emotional..31
Relationships...35
Spiritual 37

Chapter four 39
What is strategy?
Chapter five 48
What is an action step?
Why should you identify action steps?
How do you identify action steps?
 Conclusion 58

Introduction

Congratulations on stepping out and take responsibility for your life, you have taken big step towards your freedom and enjoyment. freedom from whatever holds you back and being the person, you were meant to be. After immigrating to Canada on 2002 I was under a lot of pressure and I went through depression, I was crying all day and I started to hear voices in my head. I was so frustrated and there was no hope, I was diagnosed with mental health and doctor told me I should take medication for rest of My life. I was not successful to keep any job and I had a gloomy future ahead of me, I tried so many things, but nothing seemed to be working. I studied few courses and I managed to finish them and got my diploma, but my situation never changed. I wanted to be free and change my situation badly, but I did not know how, until I got resources and tools to help me change my situation and I am grateful for that. Miracles happened, I stopped taking medication soon after. I changed my mindset because I learned that your destiny is relying on your decisions and your decisions is based on what you think. Also, your actions are based on your thoughts. my point of view has totally changed, and I believe that everything happened in my life was preparing me for this moment and present time. I believe everything works for my benefit. Do you want to be free? How badly do you want it? The tools and insights I are sharing with you will never be enough unless you match them with strong desire to be free and act upon them.

If we want something badly enough there should be nothing that can stand in the way of getting it, but the question is what do you want? Some people want to be famous badly, they do everything to be famous and they do not care about morality, they achieve their goal but at the end they are not satisfied, they use drug or alcohol or even commit suicide. Some people want to be rich badly, again they do everything to earn money, no matter what action they need to do they do it, but they are not satisfied. so, you receive something that you put your mind into but are they worth it or not?

My hope is by reading this book you will have a burning passion rise within to stand and fight for your freedom and the freedom of those to complete the book, so I researched different sources, quotes by current or historical public figures were taken from multiple public reference sources. I registered for book boot camp to get information how to write my book and I got a lot of information how to start and finish my book. because there is a lot of information on the internet, I tried to make my book around you. I love the GPS on my phone. I know I can get anywhere, even if I have never been there before. Would not be nice that we have a GPS for our life, that is what I am going to give you.

I am showing you simple and exact path that you should take to change and protect your future. I know what it is like to live in bondage and I know what it is like to live in freedom and freedom is better. Do I still have moments of worry, self-doubt and uncertainty? Yes, but I no longer live in that prison. I have found the key and my prayer is that through this knowledge you will find that same freedom for your own life. The secret to overcoming any chain, the power we have been given to fight off the lies, is Truth. If believing lies keeps us in the bondage of insecurity, then certainly believing truth is the key that sets us free and the truth is your future is on your hand, by making wise decision and this fact that everything happens for a good reason and for your benefit. I struggled all my life to find a way to grow. my motto was:

if you do not change, and today is the same as yesterday, you are like a corps.

I spend so many years alone, after graduating from university my parents passed away and my siblings immigrated so I was alone. I tried so many groups with different age, interest, and beliefs but I was still alone. I wanted to help but I did not know how and in what way I can be more useful, I studied so many courses and volunteered for years to help others just to find out what is the best way to help others, also I worked in different places with different job to find best career for myself. I fought hard to find my way in life, I cried so many days in my life and I was in desperate situation. I experienced incredibly good days and awfully bad days. There were years which I had a lot of money that I did not know how to spend it, also there was years that I needed money for food. After all these years, I found out that external situation is not important.

I am glad that I experienced those things because they made me the person who I am today. I realized that best thing I can do is share my experience to help other people, so they save a lot of time and suffering and instead enjoy their life. I had some knowledge, but I needed more information unique and make it simple to follow and apply in your life.

I hope by reading this book you get some help to organize and move forward in your life. More books coming soon, to get more information visit **www.foundationsoflife.ca**

CHAPTER ONE

Assess your situation

In this chapter I am going to talk about first step you should take to change your life and your future. Area you should consider are financial, focus, spiritual, emotional, diet, your surroundings, relationship, family, fitness, recreational and sleep pattern.

We need something that allow us to look at ourselves from a different perspective and know exactly where we are in life and how far we need to go to be the person we want to be? There is such a tool, but for many it can be difficult to find and even more difficult to use. For us to continue this battle of breaking free, we need to learn what it is and how to harness the power it can bring us. The tool is self-awareness. Having self-awareness is having a correct view of who you are. what is the truth about you? Self-awareness is the first step for all growth and development. There are two things involved here, know your limitations and flows and know your strength. my identity defined by being child of god, of course I have my limitation and I know what needs to be changed but also, I know what my strength is, I am still discovering my talents.

One of the first places we can look for self-awareness is in the mirror. The reflection of a mirror is something we take for granted today. If you are not too lazy or too cool go look in the mirror. If not now, do it the next time you are in a space with a mirror. Look at your reflection. What do you see? Do you know who are you? What are your strengths and weaknesses? What type of personality do you have? Do you like who you are? I am not just talking about your appearance. What do you feel when you look at yourself? Do you feel shame? Depression? Joy? Are you proud of yourself or disappointed? Is it hard for you to look at yourself intently? Are you able to be honest with yourself

FINANCIAL

If you look for definition of finance in the dictionary you came across this: "the science or study of the management of funds" It includes the dynamics of assets and liabilities over time under conditions of different degrees of uncertainty and risk. Where do you stand financially? are you in debt or you have financial freedom. What about your future? do you have enough money for your retirement? What do you do if something happens to you (death or disability) or in case of emergency? Do you have a financial foundation?
Foundation consists of protection, debt management, emergency fund and investment. for assessing your situation correctly first, see if you have proper protection which is insurance, next one is debt management, if you have a debt do you have a plan to manage it, next one is emergency fund, you need to have at least 3-6 month your expenses available in case of emergency, the last one is investment, if you have money you need to invest it properly.
If you do not know how to calculate your needs for future or want to know exactly how your situation is now, I have attached a form called PFS (personal financial strategy) at the back of the book for your convenience, I know it is not easy to understand financial concepts even I still learning new things. But in order to assess your situation you need to know certain things.
When I entered the financial industry first thing, I did was build a foundation for my life, first I recorded every transaction to find out my spending habit, after that I created a budget for myself.
For assessing your situation not only you need to know how much money you make and your debt but also you need to know what your expenses are.
If you want to know exactly how your spending habit is, record every transaction that you make or make arrangement to do it automatically, I made arrangement with my bank to send me any transaction that I do and I use an app to give summary of my spending. After seeing my whole month transactions there was an "aha" moment for me. I realized that I spent too much money in some area and did not put money in others area. If you are not tech savvy or you do not like technology, you can simply purchase a

notebook and a pen and record everything that you spend. In this way, you are ready for next step.

whatever your income is, it is especially important to have a budget, you should know exactly how much your income from different sources is to divide it in different category. if you do not know how much your earning is, you have no idea where your standpoint is.

Many people make the mistake that if they have enough money or a lot of money, they will have peace of mind and comfort, but it is not true because there is a lot of things that you cannot buy with money, for example happiness and friends. I am telling you this not because make you worry, whatever is your situation do not worry and do not stress yourself because your life gets better if you want to change it.

The last thing is, in what way do you earn money, do you love your work? Do you think they are paying you enough for your worth? If you answer No to any of these, then think about changing your career.

Focus

We usually associate the word focus with a sharp image, and hence with light, but the word was first applied to heat. Scientists in the 1600s chose the Latin word focus (meaning "fireplace, hearth") for the point at which rays of sunlight gathered by a magnifying glass converge and cause. But what I want to talk about is concentrating on a task like laser focus.

There is two kind of focus one of them is doing things with best quality now and the other one is stick to your goals and focus until you achieve your goals. what is quality of your job? are you distracted all the time, or you are thinking about what you are doing all the time or for some activity you do not need to think, it is your habit but are you distracted like talking to a cellphone while driving. When you are 100 percent and get the best result, you are satisfied, and your self-esteem gets higher.

Are you consistent in a thing that you are doing, or you go from one branch to another? For me it was like changing my path all the time, that is why I have lots of diploma in different areas but if I was consistent in one area, I could get a better result and every time I was changing my path, I was feeling inadequacy. after few times, I thought I am worthless, and I cannot achieve anything but that was not true. I did not have any problem completing the courses which I

studied but when I entered the reality of workforce I was discouraged and I was giving up easily, that is why I am telling you to be persistent in whatever you are doing.
For this step, I only want you to think about your situation, answer questions sincerely, it is not a test and you don't want to impress anyone, I may say it thousands time but be yourself.
What do you think about, in daily basis?
It is another problem, where is your focus? There are positive thinking and negative thinking. some people think in negative way, they always think about what if !? most of things that you are worried is not going to happen unless you focused on them for some time then it might happen. Have you heard this before " I came to whatever feared "? some people are worried about their job, their children, their money, and lot of different thing that might happen, it is not good at all, worrying is like a rocking chair it gets you move but you are not going anywhere.
are you daydreaming? If you belong to this group, you better do something, imagination is good but if you do not act is useless. some people think about where they want to go, what do they want to eat, about their future. They think about what they want to do, and this is good and bad, I will talk about it later. when you think negatively two things happen, one you attract negative things to yourself, second you are out of focus and you cannot do what you are supposed to do. To know what you think in regular basis, write your thought when you think about them right away if it is possible.

Spiritual

Spirituality refers to certain kinds of activity through which a person seeks meaning, especially a "search for the sacred". It may also refer to personal growth, blissful experience, or an encounter with one's own "inner dimension". How is your relationship with supernatural? Do you believe in supernatural? Some people say "universe", other people worship different things (you name it) but some people believe in god, although they have different version of god but all of them call him god and they believe in his power, which category are you belonging to? If you are not sure what is your beliefs, look at inside and be clear with yourself in silence. be specific, do you belong to any religion? have you ever thought about your religion; you were born in a family with certain belief, but have you ever thought about it. For now, just think clearly and be honest with yourself. If you know what your belief is, when was the last time you check up like a physical checkup, if not do it right now. As I said before, do not deny anything, be open minded and assess your current thinking and believes. Even if you do not believe in anything that is ok write "I don't believe in anything". do not let pride and prejudice prevent you from knowing the truth. Do you have any spiritual friends? To have a strong spiritual foundation we need spiritual friends around us. Emotions and spirituality are connected to each other, because of my beliefs in god I feel peace and I am happy all the time. I am connected every day to a higher power which protect me like children who are dependent to their father and I believe that everything happens for my own benefit because I believe in supervisory of god.

Emotions

When you search Wikipedia for emotion you come to this: Emotion, in everyday speech, is any relatively brief conscious experience characterized by intense mental activity and a high degree of pleasure or displeasure. Scientific discourse has drifted to other meanings and there is no consensus on a definition. Emotion is often intertwined with mood, temperament, personality, disposition, and motivation. Anger, happiness, joy, stress, and excitement are some of the feelings that are experienced in life. When we are feeling these emotions, our bodies are reacting as well. When we are nervous, we feel knots in our stomach or when we are angry the very hairs on our bodies tend to rise. Feelings can lead to harm and blissful things. When an individual is dealing with an overwhelming amount of stress and problems in their lives, it can lead them to cause self-harm. When one is in a good state of feeling they never want it to end; however, when someone is in a bad place in their life, they just want that feeling to go away or stop completely. Inflicting harm or pain to oneself is sometimes the answer for many individuals because they just want something to keep their mind off the real problem or issue that is going on in their lives. The individual figures that the pain they are causing to themselves is not as bad as what their actual problem is. These individuals cut, stab, and starve themselves in efforts to feel something other than their current feeling. Distraction is not the only reason many individuals choose to inflict self-harm. Some people inflict self-harm not to numb or distract themselves from that feeling they were feeling earlier, but they inflict self-pain to punish themselves for feeling a certain way. I remember myself years ago, when I was looking at a beautiful lady because she was beautiful, I was enjoying watching her then I was punishing myself for that feeling. I was reacting different way sometimes, I was trying to avoid going outside, sometimes I was praying hard to get rid of that feeling, both was wrong.

Are you happy (is it permanent)? What is your emotional state? are you happy or you are angry all the time. Do you feel peace and you are calm, or you are worried all the time? If you feel happiness, is it temporary or permanent? Happiness is not a matter of intensity but of balance, order and harmony." –Thomas Merton. Happiness can only be achieved if there is a balance between the physical, the mental, the spiritual and the social/emotional. Are you stressed? What do you think about, are you thinking positively or negatively, when you think are you stressed? Emotion and how do you feel is especially important because it affects all other things. Some people think that money brings happiness, but I am not agreed with this idea because I experienced both having a lot of money and not having money and my feeling was not depended on money. State of your mind controls your emotions. If you think positive all the time you are happy all the time. I want you to write what do you like about your job and what you do not like about it.

Diet and fitness

Are you healthy, or you have any disease? When was the last time you went for checkup and took some test like blood test and blood pressure and so on, what was the result? did you get any medication or recommendation, what did you do with them, did you forget about them or took your medication or advice?

How is your eating habit? do you eat healthy or you eat junk food all the time, if you eat at home what ingredients you frequently use, you eat junk food all the time, if you eat at home what ingredients you frequently use, are they frozen or fresh? Do you count how many calories do you consume or not? when you purchase something do you read labels or not? Do you understand labels? As I said in this step just assess your situation, I want you to collect information as much as you can, you need them for next step. Write down everything with specific information, for example 2 days a week eat out and the rest eat homemade food. I quit eating fast food when I realize that I am killing myself unintentionally. Right now, I exercise every day in the morning.

How many times per week do you exercise? When I say exercise, it is not necessary going to gym, how many minutes are you active (walking, doing something physical, etc.) even if you are stretching is activity. Do you sit all the time, or you have an active life? You know that it is particularly important for your health.

Doctor told one of my friends that he should be more active, and I suggest he goes for a walk every day, he said I cannot do that because weather is too cold here then I answered go to a mall and walk there. Do you make same excuses not doing something like my friend, be more active than you will be healthy and fit?

Relationship

How many friends do you have? Categorize your friend into different categories.
    Intellectual friends
    Professional friends
    Spiritual friends

Think about your friends, what class do they belong to? You need all of them and I tell you why later in next step.

How close are you with your friends? For how long do you know them?

Are you transparent in your relationships? Be honest with yourself, do you hide anything from your friends? You may not have same interest or belief with all your friends, that is why I told you categorize them, you need support from all of them to have a balanced life.

I am honest and clear with my friends, although I have different friends within different category, but I am transparent with every one of them.

Unbelievably, humans can "catch" emotions as easily as we catch colds. If you spend a lot of time with people who are happy and positive, you are more likely to feel that way yourself. If you spend a lot of time with people who are focused on negativity, that will rub off on you as well. Surround yourself with people who care for you, respect you and enrich your life.

Who do you spend your time with? How do they make you feel about yourself? Do you feel respected and validated by the people in your life? I am not suggesting that your friends and loved ones should not offer constructive critique. In fact, sometimes we need a friend to point out when we have done something thoughtless or hurtful. However, you should always feel like your loved ones approach you with kindness and respect, and you should treat them the same way.

Family

To help you with this part I give you some question to answer.
how is your relationship with your family? Do you respect your parents, grandparents, aunts and uncles? Are you in close friendship with them? How about your siblings? How is your relationship with them? How are your true feelings towards them? Do you have any anger towards them? It is easy to be mad at your family because you think they are responsible for any failure that you encountered. Search within yourself and see, do you hide anything from them, for any reason if you are not telling them the truth, you cannot be happy because you have stressed all the time and you are worried that what if they find out the truth. Write down anything that you are hiding at this point.

Recreational and sleep pattern

How much time do you spend relaxing and enjoying what you do?
For having fun, you do not need to spend a lot of money, be creative and spend fun time frequently other than spend time for an expensive trip. For example, going to the nature, sitting in a couch and close your eyes for a minute or so or play sport that you like, for some people camping and so on. If you do not love your job it is necessary to have time to relax and enjoy activities that you love how is your sleep pattern, do you sleep well, or do you have insomnia? Do you have regular sleep hours? Record your sleep hours because it affects your entire day. If you have problem with your sleep consider have a regular time for your sleep, it will help you to sleep better. I enjoy my life by being outdoor and go to the park, I always walk, and I have fun learning new things.

CHAPTER TWO

Your Goals

Congratulations you completed step one. let us move on. "Do you believe you can change? Do you believe things can be different in your life? do you know what your future looks like? I want to give you some guidance with a direction in your life. Goal Setting will help you focus on your future and maintain positive feelings associated with it.you are on a shaky place, but I want you to build a foundation, I had a lot of trouble in my life, I experienced different situation, sometimes I was so confused, occasionally I desperately needed money to survive but because I have roots and great foundation nothings can destroy me. for this reason, I want you to think again, this time about your destination, if you are honest with yourself, you know your current situation and you know your weakness. if you have a map and you know the location that you are, but you do not know where you want to go, it is useless. do you take a major journey without knowing your destination, I believe not! Why I said assess your situation, because nothing will change in your life until you know and accept the truth about your weaknesses, your relationships, your successes and failures and your past. Why is it necessary to learn the truth before anything, and you cannot change your life without it, here is why:

Behind every failure or success there is a lie or truth. If you get in debt, it is because you believed some lies like I can spend now and pay later. You overestimate your income, or you thought you can get away with it. If you are in a wrong relationship maybe you told yourself, I can change him/her. That is a lie, you cannot change anybody. If you build your life on a foundation of lies, misconceptions, deceptions, or half-truths you will never change. That is why I want you to build a solid foundation based on truth for your life. I tried so many relationships with other men and women and I found out that nobody will be changed to better person or bad person, just they show who they are after some time, and you think they have changed. they might behave better if they want to, but core values never change, unless you submit your self totally to your creator and allow him to work in your life. I get encouragement every time I pray, when you know somebody with infinite power support you and care for you, you will relax in his arm. But it needs faith. It takes me so many years to believe the fact that I am child of god and he has the best of my interest in his mind.

But still, I have doubt and I need encouragement every day to stay on track. That is why I listen to inspirational messages every day.

I was a failure and disappointed that caused bad depression and it leads to mental illness. I thought I am not going to do anything, future was totally horrified for me but one day I choose to change my future, I always wanted to learn and improve myself but there were no tools, and resource for me, I studied so many things and I tried so many things but there was no hope, I believed a lie that I am not capable of anything and god does not want to do anything for me. But one day I found the tool and resources which I am so thankful for it. You see the difference, I always wanted to change, just I was lost, and I could not find my way. That is why I wrote this book because there might be a lot of people who wants to change their situation, but they do not know how, like me.

Before Going forward, you should Recognize that life is a journey, not a destination. it is so true: life is as much about how you get where you are going as where you go. Living your life to the fullest is a process that will take your whole life to develop. Do not get frustrated if it takes you a while to learn some things, or if you experience setbacks. This is a natural part of life. Live with the purpose. Living purposefully is one of the most effortless but enjoyable experiences which you can enjoy in life. When you are living purposefully, life just flows. Like flowing water, you effortlessly adapt to any obstacle which is placed in your path. You carve out your own path for life as you pass peacefully through. There are times when things can become turbulent and you can fall off purpose but with a small amount of conscious effort, you can usually guide yourself back, until you are living purposefully once again. It may take a little time and effort to find your purpose but once you do so, and you choose to live your purpose, the benefits are beyond measure. For me it took years to find my purpose in life, I always wanted to help others, I did not know how I can be more useful but now I am certain what is my purpose. Dishonesty saps away energy and happiness. When we are not honest with ourselves, we hold ourselves back from learning and growth. When we are not honest with others, we damage trust and intimacy.

We may be dishonest for a variety of reasons. Research has shown that sometimes we lie because we are jealous and want to hurt others. Sometimes, we lie because we are afraid, we will be hurt if we reveal the truth, or we are afraid of a confrontation. It can be hard to be honest, especially with yourself, but doing so will help you live a fuller, richer life. All too often, we spend a lot of time looking at what we do not like about ourselves, what we would like to change, what we think should be different. Spending all your time focused on what you do not like or what happened in your past means that you cannot focus on your future. Make a conscious decision to learn to love yourself, just as you are.

Make a list of your strengths. What are you good at? These can be lofty achievements, such as inventing a new technology, or "everyday" skills, such as being friendly to others. Paying attention to what your strengths are can help you continue to develop them without considering yourself as a failure. to me it is like my nature to be kind and helpful to others and it is my strength also I have high tolerance.

Set goals that are meaningful to you, and do not compare them to anyone else's. If a personally meaningful goal is to learn to play your favorite song on the guitar, do not feel bad if you do not become a Rock star guitarist. I always wanted to help and serve others, that is why I studied social worker and volunteered for many years, but the problem was I did not know specifically what exactly I want, how can I be more useful to others until now, I have experienced a lot in my life and gain a lot of knowledge and helped a lot of people, so I want to transfer my knowledge and experience to others with love.

Keep your goals performance based. Achieving your goals takes hard work, dedication, and motivation. However, you need to make sure that you can achieve your goals through your effort. but I am not saying stop there. You can congratulate yourself for your effort and move on. I went to film school and studied acting because I wanted to make a difference by sending messages through my films. As I told you before I always wanted to make an impact, but I did not know how. Your core values are the beliefs that shape who you are and how you live your life. They may be spiritual beliefs or simply deeply held beliefs that are important to you. Reflecting on your values will help you set goals for yourself that are "value-congruent," meaning in line with your values. You are more likely to feel fulfilled and happy

when you are living in accordance with your values.
Stand up for what you believe in and do not let others push you around. It is possible to do this and still be open to other people's ideas, as they may surprise you. Sometimes, society confounds self-criticism with helping yourself improve. However, much research shows that the more hostile and critical you are of yourself, the more likely you are to be the same way toward others. Negative self-talk and self-criticism do not help you become a better person or achieve your goals. Try self-kindness and self-compassion instead. If you do not love yourself and you are not at peace with yourself, you cannot do anything. For example, if you find yourself consistently telling yourself what is wrong with you or what you do not like about yourself, be purposeful and challenge those thoughts with positive ones. Replace thoughts like "I'm such a loser" with "That situation didn't go exactly the way I'd planned. I'll go back to the drawing board and think of another way to approach it." I had problem getting attention from people and every time that I was approaching someone and got rejected, I was thinking what is wrong with me? Nobody wants me!!? Then I realized that there is nothing wrong with me, some people do not like me that is all. This is normal, nobody is loved by everybody, some people hate you and some loves you.
Try to think logically about your self-criticisms. Criticizing ourselves can be all too easy. The next time you notice yourself being harsh, try to find a rational response to that criticism. For example, if you found yourself thinking "I'm so dumb, I don't know anything in this class and everyone's smarter than I am," examine that thought logically. Is everyone smarter than you, or are some individuals just more prepared for the material than others? Is your performance in the class related to your intellect (not likely) or is it because you may not have the preparation you needed to excel? Are you studying effectively? Would you benefit from a tutor? Breaking things down in this logical manner can help you figure out steps to take to help yourself improve without writing yourself off.
One of the reasons we become frustrated is that we expect things to stay the same. However, life is full of change. Open yourself to the processes of change and growth and learn to adapt to the new situations and challenges that happen. Fostering positive emotions, such as happiness and optimism, will help you develop flexibility. Look for patterns in how you respond to events and situations.

Determine what is helpful and what is not. This can help you learn to modify the responses that are not helpful and learn to be more adaptive. Not only will you feel better yourself, but you will also be able to better interact with others. Learn to look at "negative" events as learning experiences instead. Looking at setbacks or situations that appear as negative as "failures" can lead you to obsess over them, rather than learn and grow from them. Rather than seeing a challenge or roadblock as a negative, see it as a positive space for learning and improvement.

For example, J.K. Rowling, the author of the phenomenally successful Harry Potter series, has said that she sees failure as incredibly beneficial, something to be valued rather than feared. A goal is a desired result that a person plans and commits to achieve: a personal desire endpoint in some sort of assumed development. Many people endeavor to reach goals within a finite time by setting deadlines. Spend sometimes and think about what you want to achieve, think big, there is a magic in thinking big, do not limit yourself but be realistic at the same time. Schwartz argues that the main thing holding people back is the relative smallness of their thoughts, and he emphasizes the importance of Thinking positively toward oneself. We have been conditioned to think small, not to be greedy, and to overall expect less and demand less from life. We have been taught that we should be happy and thankful with what we have and that there are many others less fortunate than ourselves. I am totally agreed with this, I am grateful for what I have, and I spend a lot of my time helping others I have been in both sides, being rich and not having enough money for essentials and I am happy that I experienced those because I know I can be happy no matter my situation is, but I think big and I dream big all the time.

Do not limit yourself about number of your goals, brainstorm in every area and write down whatever you want to achieve, after then you can take a good look at them and see which one of them is based on true values and Prioritize them. There is so much I want to do, even I wrote them down, but there is no way I can do them all so I should pick some of them based on priority. Imagination is also especially important, when you want to create your goals, see what could be changed. visualization add value to your plans.

Take a good look at your behavior and your thought, look back and review your life, if you see any change in your life what was the reason for that, record everything and put them together. What are you pretending to be, have you pretended that you are someone else or you have quality or character that you do not have.

Imagination is concerned with both tangible and intangible aspects of our lives, unlike visualization where only tangible aspects are considered. Also, imagination does not necessarily require previous knowledge. Unlike visualization, imagination is not always concerned about the details. It is more "in the moment", so to speak. For example, if you are imagining playing in the rain, you are more concerned about the experience itself rather than anything else.

After you wrote down your brainstorming, learn how to set SMART goals. (specific, measurable, attainable, relevant, and time-bound) because dreams do not work unless they have a deadline, be specific, achievable, and you can measure them, for example if you want to lose weight you should know exactly how many pounds or kilo you want to lose and when is the deadline to achieve it. In this way, you can measure if you achieve that goal or not, of course it should be attainable, for example if you say I want to lose 100 pound in one month it is not realistic.

The process of setting goals helps you choose where you want to go in life. By knowing precisely what you want to achieve, you know where you should concentrate your efforts. You will also quickly spot the distractions. Goal setting is a powerful process for thinking about your ideal future, and for motivating yourself to turn your vision of this future into reality. First consider what you want to achieve, and then commit to it.Many people feel as if they are lost in the world. They work hard, but they do not seem to get anywhere worthwhile. A key reason that they feel this way is that they did not spent enough time thinking about what they want from life and have not set themselves any goals.

I met a lot of people who are aimlessly wake up every morning and after doing their daily tasks they go to bed and they are like this all their life. I was like this for few years, I was depressed, so I did not motivate to do anything, my day was like getting up in the morning , have lunch mid-day go to bed again until next morning , of course this is extreme, but some people go to work , come back watch television , have food and sleep, this routine goes on and on .

Goals are always hard to set, and much harder to accomplish. Most of us wake up in the morning and let the events of the day dictate our time and behaviors. You can control everything inside even outside, but not precisely, every one of us experience different emotions but it is our choice how to react. And if you think positive, good things happens to you too.

Why Set Goals? Top-level athletes, successful businesspeople, and achievers in all fields all set goals for themselves. Setting goals gives you long-term vision and short-term motivation. It focuses your acquisition of knowledge and helps you to organize your time and your resources so that you can make the very most of your life.

By setting sharp, clearly defined goals, you can measure and take pride in the achievement of those goals, and you will see forward progress in what might previously have seemed a long pointless grind. You will also raise your self-confidence, as you recognize your own ability and competence in achieving the goals that you have set.

* First you create your "big picture" of what you want to do with your life (for example the next 10 years) and identify the large-scale goals that you want to achieve.
* Then, you break these down into the smaller and smaller targets that you must hit to reach your lifetime goals.
* Finally, once you have your plan, you start working on it to achieve these goals.

I want to achieve a lot of things in my life, that is why I have a big list, but I cannot work on all of them I need to prioritize and therefore, you should start the process of setting goals by looking at your lifetime goals. Then, you work down to the things that you can do, say, the next five years, then next year, next month, next week, and today, to start moving towards them. The first step in setting personal goals is to consider what you want to achieve in your lifetime (or at least, by a significant and distant age in the future). Setting lifetime goals gives you the overall perspective that shapes all other aspects of your decision making.

Top-level athletes, successful businesspeople, and achievers in all fields all set goals. By setting sharp, clearly defined goals, you can measure and take pride in the achievement of those goals, and you will see forward progress in what might previously have seemed a long pointless grind. You will also raise your self-confidence, as you recognize your own ability and competence in achieving the goals that you have set. Your goals might change along the way, but you are closer to your goals anyway even if you change your goals, for example I wanted to establish nonprofit organization, that was my goal because I wanted to help others, but I changed my goals because I realized that I can be more useful, and it is more attainable to have coaching company instead. Although I changed my goal, but I am closer to what I want. purpose or aim is the anticipated result which guides reaction, or an end, which is an object, either a physical object or an abstract object, that has value. It might be inward or outward based on your goals.as I said before to create your goals you should know your values because sometimes you want to achieve something which is unworthy or it is not real goal, what is your values? If you want to achieve something to impress others that is wrong even if you want to be friend or get married with someone and you want to reach certain goal to get closer to that person it is totally wrong, always improve yourself and right partner will come to you.

first you need to build a foundation like a house, without foundation you cannot build something on the top. the other thing is our culture or norm of society, sometimes we follow the crowd, and we do not ask ourselves is it true? For example, if you are overweight, do you want to lose weight because everybody says have a slim body is good or you want to improve your health.it is easy to cheat ourselves but it is not going to work if you are not truly honest about your values. How you always act is coordinated with the most fundamental values and your beliefs. What you say is not evidence but your behaviors and your choices, especially in time of anger or stress shows what are your fundamental believes.

For example, I was under a lot of pressure or anxiety or anger but never use bad words because it is my core believe that you should not say bad word from your mouth which you praise god with that mouth, they are not coming together. What you say even in jokes shows that what is in your heart. Change requires new thinking. To change, you must learn the truth and start making good choices, but you also must change the way you think.

The way you think determines the way you feel, and the way you feel determines the way you act. If you want to change the way you act, you start by changing the way you think. In addition, if you want to change the way you feel, you must start with the way you think. Analysis the past, how many goals did you have before which they are not your goals anymore, So, your goals might not your goals in 5 years anymore, then when you want to create your goals for long term think about this fact as well. Do not follow society, Definition of some words change during time, like being cool, when you are a teenager being cool is different than being cool in age of 30, anyway meaning of cool determines by society and I do not think following society makes you any good. One of life's biggest ironies is how often people complain about their circumstances, yet rarely do nothing about them. It is not that they do not have good intentions, or the desire for change is not great. It is that change is scary and risky. Even when we are unhappy with our current situation, we are familiar with it. Change is just so unknown! I heard an exceptionally good example for this, somebody said I do not want to change my shoes because my old shoes are comfortable for me if I change my shoes, I must adapt to new one, that is how change works, you must adapt to new things that are not comfortable for you .

I read somewhere that, as an experiment, someone put two ads in a newspaper. They were for the same job, doing the same work with the same hours, but one of them offered to pay a salary many times the other. Guess what? About ten times more people applied for the lower paid job! People think small. And that is one of the reasons they fail. I am totally agreed with not being greedy and be happy with what you have, also help others, because if you want more you never will be happy, we always say that if I get that job, if I marry that person, if …. I will be happy. When you get what, you wanted you always want more and if you do not appreciate and thankful for what you have, you never attract more.

Envy does not get us anywhere, instead of comparing and looking what other people have, look at yourself and what you have and be thankful for that.

Most people are afraid of thinking big, they are scared to be successful, scared to be rich. For most people, being rich is a pleasant dream, but they are comfortable with the dream – it is nice, and it makes them feel good. But hugely successful and wealthy people take it to the next level – they are committed to being rich, to being successful, and they are prepared to keep on keeping on until the dream becomes reality. Also, there is the law of sowing and reaping and it is one of the universal laws. It is the law of cause and effect. Whatever you sow and plant in the garden will produce a crop. For every cause, there is a corresponding effect. Use this law to your advantage. You are going to manage what you sow, and you are going to manage what you reap. What you sow is a cause, what you reap is an effect. You are sowing in your life and other person's life, if you want any change in your life you should act differently. Law of attraction says if you want to receive, give. By sowing in another person's life, you reap more. But the problem is if you managed to be rich, do not forget where you come from and keep giving and do not be afraid of losing your money.

There is a quote I love, which summarizes all of this:
"Our worst fear is not that we are inadequate; our deepest fear is that we are powerful beyond measure. It is our light, not our darkness that most frightens us. We ask ourselves, 'Who am I to be brilliant, gorgeous, talented and fabulous?' Who are you not to be? You are a child of God; you are playing small does not serve the world. There is nothing enlightened about shrinking so that other people will not feel insecure around you. We were born to make manifest the glory of God within us. It is not just in some of us, it is in everyone, and as we let our own light shine, we unconsciously give other people permission to do the same. As we are liberated from our own fear, our presence automatically liberates others." But it is our choice, we have free will that let god works in our life or not.

At this point, we spend a great deal of time dreaming of what we would like to be different. Whether it is losing weight, starting a new job, finding romance, or finally writing that book, we are too busy to stop and figure out how to get there. We are dreaming--not planning--and we know that all change requires work, the thought of which is simply exhausting. I spent a lot of planning to write this book, I had to make sure what do I want to do with this book, and I was thinking about it, but I was planning not only dreaming. I talked about thinking big and believe in yourself, that is true but at the same time you should be humble and the reason I say humbly because we do not want to admit what is not working in our lives because of pride. I have met a lot of people who do not have any money but pretend to be rich or a lot of people afraid of showing themselves as truly as they are because they do not want people think about them or judge them bad. if you are one of them, at least be honest with yourself and admit that you have some problems.

sometimes we worry. What if we go through all the work to make a change, and it does not work out? Or even worse, what if it is not what we want after all? Edwin Locke, one of the foremost researchers in goal setting, states that the No. 1 thing that stands in the way of goal attainment is fear. Fear of failure, fear of success, fear of the unknown, fear of making the wrong decision, looking foolish, being embarrassed and so on.

Carolyn Adams-Miller, author of Creating Your Best Life List, says that when we engage in a well-planned risk, even if it is scary, we immediately gain confidence, progress toward goal accomplishment and an increase in our life satisfaction. Even when the risk does not turn out exactly as hoped, we still benefit. We learn that we can handle whatever curveballs life throws at us and increase our resiliency (the ability to bounce back after disappointment). There is saying that if life gives you lemon, make lemonade that means, use the best of what you have and try to find any opportunity to learn from any situation. Together, these experiences increase our inner strength and lead us to be more willing to try new and different experiences in the future. And that what makes life exciting. I am doing this recently, when I am stuck in traffic, I think it is good opportunity to practice patience.

You cannot change if you do not know what you want to change, I had a lot of problems still have some, but I had to admit that I have problem and be humble to accept my flaws. All of us has blind spot that I am going to talk about it later.   Where do you stand financially? Are you confident you will have the money you need for the things that are important in your life? The first step in planning for the future is defining where you are now. Express your goals positively, for example if you want to make wiser decisions do not say do not make stupid mistakes, write down make wiser decision and in planning section choose strategy to help you make wiser decision.

think about different aspects that you assessed in previous chapter, if you know what you really want to write them down. As a reminder, different categories, you should consider are financial, focus, your surroundings, spiritual, emotional, diet, relationship, family, fitness, recreational, sleep pattern.

Financial goals

Your financial goals are depended on your situation but there are some necessary steps you should take no matter what your income is, first you should check your beliefs about money, some people thinks that money is roots of all evil. NO !! money is the tool you can use it in a good way or bad way, if you are attached to money or classify people based on money they have, you should change it. People's worth is not based on money, even I do not like (low class and high class) there is no such a thing. I do not value money, to me money is a tool to reach my goals and every time I needed money it came to me miraculously, or I did not have to pay money for that thing. Anyway, money is not a bad thing and if you want to have a lot of money you should be generous and give then you will receive it abundantly also Think like a rich person and learn how to earn money.

If you are in debt, your goal should be financial freedom, I tell you how in following chapters. Most of us do not wait to become a statistic to know that we are in trouble. It is ironic that we live in one of the wealthiest countries in the world, but we always have money problems. Debt has become a way of life. Nobody teaches us how to manage our money in school. Financial issues are not often discussed, and financial products not always explained. To have a solid financial foundation you should have protection, you never know what is going to happen in the future so you should be prepared specially if you want to have same lifestyle or better that you have right now. There is a lot of product out there, but you need an advisor to help you in this matter, but there is a lot of resources to educate yourself. We use credit cards every day and do not always understand all the hidden charges. There is a jungle of complex rules and regulations for the thousands of stocks, bonds, funds, savings plans, credit cards and loans out there.

We need to change, and the task will not be easy, but we need understanding first. The old days of passive dependence must end; a new era of financial freedom must begin. The best I can hope for is to get your attention and interest into financial matters and to obtain some basics of how money works. Remember nobody interested in your financial situation more than yourself and you cannot depend on government or your employer. 30 percent of Canadians cannot handle more than 500 dollars of unexpected expenses. The rest of the world are not doing better. More than ever, people need to change their thinking from social security to self-security.

If you were to qualify for the maximum monthly retirement pension at age of 65 it would be 1.065 per month. Is this enough to provide you with the secure retirement that you desire? I told you, there are some necessary steps, because like building a house you should start with a solid financial foundation and build it from ground up.
First, you should have proper protection in the event of disability, health problems, or premature death. You should reduce your liability and get out of death. You should set aside 3 to 6 months of your income to deal with sudden changes in your job or business. And you should save and invest for the long run.

Focus

Next goal should be your focus, there is two kind of focus one of them is goal setting and planning which solve half of your problem because you know where you are going and if you stick to the plan you are not distracted and you are focusing on your plan. But you must know when go forward and when to stop, maybe that goal does not serve you anymore. the other part of the problem which is being now and focus on the task that you are doing needs a bit more effort because we are not accustomed to stay in the moment, I have a challenge in this area, there are two situations, one of them is when you want to do a task alone, the other one is when you are in a group.
 If you are doing something alone your goal should be stay put and continue doing that task while you are not thinking about something else. If you attend a meeting or doing something with a group, the only challenge is do not think about something else and contribute to the group.

Surroundings

Your surroundings are also important because if you live or work in a clean and organize place you feel better and more relaxed, if you are not organized, one of your goals should be clean and organize your house or office including all your files. Part of your surroundings are people around you, where do you stand with your relationships? How close are you with your friends and family? Important thing is how is your relationship with yourself, what image do you have about yourself, Are you in peace with yourself and your past.

think about your past and figure out why things happened in the past that you understand it now and what happened that you do not understand. There is a reason behind Everything that happened in your life, people who came into your life and left you, good experiences and bad experiences, even bad experiences occurred for your own good, think about it for a moment. Your goals should be forgiving all your friends and family, if you have any problem with them clear it and ask for forgiveness.

CHAPTER THREE

Physical, emotional, and spiritual Goals

Y ou know your situation, now it is the time to set goals to improve your health and fitness. In terms of diet there is a lot of plan for diet, but you do not need any of them if you do what am I going to tell you. First, you need to eat at home, if you are outside all the time or for your lunch if you are at work, prepare something in advance. This is first step, then you can change type of food are you eating each day, you should have a well-balanced diet. Having a well-balanced diet is one of the most important parts of maintaining a generally healthy body. Without a balanced diet, it will be exceedingly difficult to maintain proper health. A balanced diet means that you consume foods from each food group, in addition, you should consume a variety of foods within each food group. Having a wide variety of foods from food groups will allow you to consume a variety of different nutrients.

Lastly, a balanced diet means eating the right proportions or servings of each food. If you eat mostly protein foods but very few fruits or vegetables, your diet is not balanced. Balance your meals and snacks during the day. Aim for three to four servings of protein daily, five to nine servings of fruits and vegetables, and three to four servings of grains. By now you have noticed what are four groups of food, they are (fruits and vegetables, grains, dairy products, meat, and proteins) It is a good idea to Monitor calories. To have a generally healthy body, you should try to maintain a healthy weight. If you are overweight, you are not maintaining a generally healthy body. Calories are a unit of measurement. You eat calories from food and that energy is used to fuel your bodily functions and activities throughout the day.

If you consume too many calories you may run the risk of gaining weight. If you do not eat enough calories you may lose weight. approximately you need a 2,000 calorie-per-day diet. You may need to change how many calories you eat daily to match your body's needs and to maintain a healthy weight. To lose weight, it is considered safe to cut 500 calories from your diet and aim to lose about one to two pounds per week. I do not like counting calories, if you are like me Use an online calculator or smartphone app to find out how many calories your body needs. A good rule of thumb is that a moderately active adult needs about 15 calories per pound to maintain weight. Track calories to see if your current diet meets your needs.

I told you that I do not like counting calories and I encountered several plans that suggest servings and exact number of calories that you should take, even when I exercise app that I am using tells me how much calories did I burned. Because I want to help everybody, from so disciplined person to lousy person, I told you about calories you should take for disciplined person and for people who does not want to trouble themselves counting calories just do not eat fast food and cook at home. now I tell my personal experience , I was eating outside all the time until I realized that I am killing myself so I stopped eating outside and found a solution not to eat junk food anymore but that was not enough because I was purchasing prepared or frozen food and warm it at home, it was a progress but that was not good either, so I decide to cook myself but I hate cooking, I searched a lot recipe and a lot of apps to help me prepare a food at home but it was time consuming , if you have time I suggest make a meal plan and prepare your food at home then you can enjoy restaurant food from time to time. You do not need to count calories if you do not want to but read the labels when you want to buy something then decide to buy it or not. I am not eating out unless I should do it.

The other part of healthy body is exercise, to set a fitness goal you should consider some fact like other areas. How big is the goal? Is your goal attainable in three months or more? If it is long term goal and you need to spend longer time to achieve that goal, I suggest you break down your goal into smaller goals, then it is easier to get motivated because you achieve success soon then you can go after another goal. Be realistic about what time you should devote to the goal and be honest about your fitness level. one of your goals should be exercise at least 3 days per week. I exercise daily because I am used to it and it is part of my daily routine. if you are overweight or you are facing stress, exercise is essential. You can manage your time to exercise and you do not need to go to the gym and pay membership fees, you can exercise at home. There is a lot of apps or online program. As a rule, never increase your weight lifted or your minutes exercised by more than 10 percent in any given week. Slow and steady does win the race!

your goals should be specific and measurable for example if you want to lose weight you should state how many pounds or kilograms you want to lose and specify when. You cannot set your goal as being healthier which is not measurable for each of these goals you should be specific and define it.

For me increase Strength and flexibility has priority so my exercise plan include activity with focus on this two. To be specific I should say my goal is lift 50 pounds and be flexible so I can bend and hold my toes, I should work on these two goals.

Emotional

Would you like to be in a good mood every day? You are probably thinking, Yes, of course I would. Who would not? I spent a lot of years being controlled by a variety of moods and believing I had no choice in how I felt. Then I finally learned that our mind, mouth, moods and attitudes are all intricately connected. First you think, and then your thoughts turn into words that you speak, and the two of them together affect you emotionally and turn into moods and attitudes.

Although we do not always have the power to change every unpleasant circumstance in our lives, we do have the power to change our reaction and our point of view. Nobody enjoys a troubling or painful circumstance, but I have found if we look at it in a hopeful, faith-filled way, we can watch God work all things out for our good. Enjoying life begins with the thoughts you choose to think. Yes, it is that simple! No matter what is going on in your life today, if you will choose happy, hope-filled thoughts you will feel happier. Our thoughts are directly connected to our feelings, so if we want to feel better, we need to think better.

Think of the mind like the gas tank in your automobile. Your automobile will run well, or perhaps not even run at all, depending on what kind of fuel you put into it. In the same way, when you choose your thoughts carefully, your quality of life will improve in amazing ways! Be honest with yourself and think about what you have been mentally focusing on and how you have been feeling emotionally. I feel certain you will see a definite connection. Nothing good comes from thinking sour, critical, and negative thoughts, but something good always comes when we think according to God's plan for our life. Renewing our mind, mouth, moods and attitudes is not always easy, but it is possible. I have personally been working toward this goal for years, and although I have not arrived at perfection, I have made amazing progress. I have successful days, and I also have days when I feel like I have failed miserably. If you desire greater emotional stability, and the ability to maintain a consistent good attitude no matter what your circumstances are, then make it a goal and do not give up until you have reached it.

I always start my days with thanking god and declare that this is an exceptionally good day then I get a quiet moment to receive a message. after that I exercise based on my plan and goals I want to achieve. That is why I feel good all the time and I am prepared to face any challenge during the day.

Do good things happen in your life by chance? Some seem to think so; however, I know that when you think of things in a specific way, good things start to happen. This means that good things happen because of action and not because of chance. Our thoughts determine our future, and the key is to pay attention to your internal dialogue.

What is your internal dialogue? Your internal dialogue is that voice inside your head which commentates on everything around you. It is the voice that applies your logic and reasoning to situations. For example, your internal dialogue allows you to:

    1. make decisions about things like how something makes you feel

2. form an opinion on something
3. decide if you believe something or not
4. know whether to do a certain thing or not
5. know if you should change what you are doing

It is non-stop and continually shapes your world how you see it. Depending on what your internal dialogue says at key points in your life will determine not only how you feel about certain things but also what you believe about yourself and things around you and this will determine to your body where best to spend your energy. your internal dialogue runs automatically if you let it however, if you pay attention to it, you can choose what you say to yourself.

The link between thoughts and feelings, when you are happy the muscles in your cheeks contract causing you to smile. Similarly, if you contract the muscles in your cheeks and you smile, this causes you to feel happy: they are both causally linked.

This link is also true between what you think and what you feel. If you feel bad, it will be because you are thinking negative thoughts and if you feel good you will be thinking positive thoughts. These are generally unconscious (automatic); however, by paying attention to your thoughts you bring them into conscious (manual) awareness and can change them. Are you in control of your feelings? Or your feelings control you? technique of listening will be of use to you and will give you an insight as to why this may be dominating your life. Once you have an awareness of what you are saying to yourself, you will find that thinking positively becomes much easier. Choose your thoughts wisely, once you fully accept what you think you can control how you feel, if you are worried about something, you do not have to repeat that thought, change the channel. Think other way about best thing might happen.

On the other hand, if you become aware of thoughts that are making you feel sad, decide to learn from them and change your thoughts; look at the positive side of things that will make you feel happy and empowered and your behaviour will start to reflect that. Over time you will install this positive thinking as a habit and will most likely start smiling at people and complementing them which will improve your personality and will ultimately determine your future.

It is normal to have negative thought but if they are unresolved for prolonged periods, they are not good. The next time you feel negative about something I would like you to pay attention to what you are thinking and just for fun, think the opposite and make it 10 times bigger and better and see how it makes you feel. So, if you have no money, think about being very wealthy. If you have just split up with a partner, think what it would be like meeting someone with all the qualities you personally desire. If you are feeling lonely and fed up with your friends, imagine what it would be like in your ideal world, what qualities would you want your friends to have? Feeling positive will cause positive things to happen. It is the fundamental to the law of attraction. Don't depend on your money or your power to be happy, I experienced both I had power, I was part of management team in a factory that I am shareholder, everybody respecting me as their boss, it felt good and when I was in university I was part of theatre group and we performed in different event for organizations, one time I went to buy train tickets, clerk was excited to see me and he told his co-worker that I am the one who performed for them, I felt like a celebrity . These feelings are good, but we should not be happy based on external situation because they are temporary, and it can change anytime.

Forgiveness is good for your body and your soul. Forgiving can be incredibly difficult, but it also reduces stress, decreases your blood pressure, and lowers your heart rate. Forgiveness can help you feel fulfilled and happy even if the other person never acknowledges the wrongdoing. Think about whatever it is you want to forgive. Notice how those thoughts make you feel. Accept those feelings; judging them or trying to repress them will only make it worse. Transform that painful experience into a learning experience. What could you have done differently? What can you learn from this experience that can help you become a better person now? Remember that you can only control your actions, not others'. One of the reasons forgiveness is so hard is because it's entirely dependent on you. The other person may never acknowledge the wrongdoing. S/he may never face consequences or learn from the experience. However, holding on to your anger about the situation ultimately only hurts you. Learning to forgive, regardless of whether the other person takes any action or experiences any result, will help you heal.

Forgiving yourself is as important as forgiving others. When we dwell on things about our past lives or behavior that we regret, we can end up falling into an unproductive cycle of self-blame, rather than using those experiences as tools to help us focus on becoming better people in the present. Use the techniques such as challenging negative self-talk and practicing mindfulness, to help you forgive yourself and show yourself the same compassion you show others. While forgiving remember we need to forget certain situations in life which brought us negative emotions. I know this is so difficult but as you grow things that hurts you before they are not important to you anymore and you do not remember certain things.

Another thing you should consider to be happy is do you love what you do? If not consider your option to change your career, how do you do that? If you want to find the career for you, a good first step is to find out what makes you happy. But sometimes we do not know what makes us happy because we have never tried it before. Open yourself up to new experiences and you might surprise yourself. Break down why you enjoy what you do. Identify the jobs that you like and what it is exactly about your dream career that you find so captivating. Really break it down to its key element. Not everyone can be something like a rock star or a famous artist, but there is more than one job that lets you enjoy the fun part of it.

For example, if you want to be a rock star, is it that you enjoy being the center of attention? Maybe you enjoy creating things. Or maybe it is getting to listen to music. There are more accessible careers that let you do these things! Follow that passion. Once you find out what specific thing it is that makes you feel happy and fulfilled, follow that passion until you have a career that is focused on doing that thing. If you are doing work that caters to your passion, then you will love getting up every morning and you will not feel awful when you go to bed at night.

Find out how to succeed. Find out what you need to do in order to get the career you want and then work to do that. Look for advertisements for your ideal job and look at the requirements they want. Do not feel restricted by what you see: there are ways to go back to school, even if money is a problem.

Keep moving forward. Keep going, keep working your way up, and never, ever give up. Keep giving yourself new goals. As soon as you stop working to be better than you feel unfulfilled and bored. Accept change. Change is going to happen, whether you want it to or not. If you spend a lot of energy and build a lot of stress trying to fight changes, you are never going to be happy. Accept changes, even if they are bad ones. If something is bad happen, you can always find a way to fix the problem or make it better. But you do not want to fight a blessing in disguise.

Appreciate the good things. When good things happen to you, you should celebrate them and enjoy every moment of them, instead of worrying about when you will lose them or just wanting more. This will maximize the enjoyment that you get out of life. Money is good to have, but once our basic needs and savings goals are met, it is time to stop earning more and more. Letting go of the need for money just for the sake of it has been fulfilling experience for me. I do not own my money that is why I do not have any stress losing it.

Relationships

I told you about your friends and family, now it is the time to set your goals for having better relationships with your friends and family. Traditionally, we build friendships based on proximity. Social psychology shows us that we tend to have a greater fondness for those whom we spend more time with. We often build these friendships at a young age but as we change and our lives change, these relationships fail to change with us. Thus, we can end up spending a great deal of time with people who no longer support our growth as human beings. When you are living purposefully, you understand the need to evaluate relationships to ensure that they are mutually supportive. It is not just about what others can do for you it is also important that you can help others. the objective is to organize your priorities.

If the crowd is doing wrong, make it less crowded. Easier said than done, right? Peer pressure can be also being a terrible reality. Few students want to stand out and be alone, especially if they might lose friends. Any friend that asks you to compromise something that you believe in is probably not as good of friend as you think. Facing peer pressure is having the ability to do what is right even though it is not popular. The key to this is to determine your standards and boundaries before a situation arises. It is so difficult to make the right choice in the heat of the moment. It works in every kind of relationship and in every age, range including marriage, one of your goals should be setting standard and boundaries for yourself and your partner or friend, then you know that how you should react in case of conflict or argue even crisis.

I made a lot of mistakes in the past because of peer pressure and made some poor choices and tried to connect with wrong peoples because I wanted to avoid loneliness or to be popular. I assure you being popular or have a lot of money does not make you happy, if you want to be friend with someone in power or someone with a lot of money or get married to someone rich just because of power or money, that is totally wrong. And if you have money or power and people wants to be your friend just because of what you have you should avoid them. Learning to communicate assertively (but not aggressively) can help you feel stronger, more confident, and more fulfilled. Assertive communication acknowledges that both you and others have needs and works to give everyone a way to be heard.

Be open and honest, but do not use judging or blaming language. If someone has hurt you, it is healthy to share your feelings with him or her. However, do not use language that puts blame on the other person, such as "You were so unkind to me" or "You don't even care about my needs. "Use "I"-statements. Using statements that focus on what you are feeling and experiencing keep you from sounding blaming or judging. For example, "I felt hurt when you talked to me like that." I felt like my needs were not important to you."

When you are living purposefully, you do not run away from your problems. You do not blame others for what has gone wrong in your life.

You accept full responsibility for results which you achieve. When you do not get the results, you desire, you identify the changes that you can make and put a plan in place to make those changes. Give constructive criticism and accept it from others. Do not simply tell others to do or not to do something. Explain why you are asking. Invite others to share their needs and ideas with you. Use cooperative language, such as "What would you like to do?" or "What do you think?"

Instead of automatically feeling a need to assert your own point of view, try saying something like "Tell me more" when you hear something that at first seems like something you would normally disagree with. Try to see from his/her point of view. Be selfless in your attitude towards others. One of the biggest things that holds us back in our lives is our focus on the idea that we "deserve" certain things. This feeling can result in feelings of dissatisfaction and anger. Give love without expecting it to be returned. Love others even when it is hard. This does not mean you should be a doormat for those who do not treat you right. You can love and accept someone and still recognize that they are not good for you. You can still avoid that person but still love everybody. Believe it or not, love is helpful even in the workplace. Workplaces that foster a culture that includes compassion, caring, and expressions of affection are more productive and have more satisfied workers.

Spiritual

The purpose of any goal is the same: to have an objective on which you can focus, for which you can strive. A goal is an outcome that you want to happen, that you are willing to work towards. Spiritual goals are no different from any other goals: it is like setting a target up for yourself, it helps mark the direction for which you want to aim. Goals are your own business to determine. A good place to start is to ask yourself where you want to be in a year, or in 5 or 10 years. Another good idea for goals is to plan specific things you want to do to explore, nurture or practice your spirituality. According to Educational Psychology Interactive, spiritual goals are tools that aid people in reaching self-fulfillment and transcendence based on Maslow's hierarchy of human needs. The hierarchy of human needs lists physiological needs as the most important, followed by safety, acceptance and belonging. Spiritual goals assist people in fulfilling several of these basic needs by providing a social network and sense of belonging within the community. How many of us set spiritual goals? It is interesting that many desires to keep their physical bodies strong and healthy, but neglect their spirits? We challenge our muscles at the gym by increasing reps and increasing the weight used. Do we do this with our spirits?

While no one can tell you what your spiritual goals should be, I can offer some suggestions that might point you in the right direction:

- Explore your own beliefs. Think of the biggest questions you want answered and determine you will spend the next few months researching, reflecting, and meditating on answers. Keep a notebook or a journal as a record for this endeavor, so you can write down your evolving thoughts and feelings. For me praying and study word of god every day is essential because I want to know god more and become more like him.
- Plan to incorporate quiet time to in your life to think about spirituality. I do not mean big, formal rites of any faith system; I mean small, daily acts that pertain to your spirituality. Reading spiritual books are a great way to get the mind used to switching into that spiritual mode. Plan to keep up small but meaningful efforts, such as mealtime prayers, evening meditation, scripture reading. Setting spiritual goals does not require attending formal religious services. Spiritual goals are often determined by examining a personal ethical or moral code and making changes to improve that code. For instance, setting the goal of giving back to the community, is accomplished by volunteering at local charities or non-profit organizations. Spiritual goals allow people to identify their personal beliefs and determine whether current goals match those beliefs.
- Search for and join a group. This can be a church, but it does not have to be. The focus of the group should be spiritual, a practice with which you are comfortable. Having a group, though, can be a great motivator and help keep you on track.
- Begin to practice what you preach. If you admire Buddhist monks for their discipline in their daily routine and patience, start your own routine and work on your own patience. Start living the life you want to live, that you think is right to live.

Every now and then, you may want to re-evaluate your spiritual goals to see how far you have come, and how far you need to go. Change will not happen overnight but start making small changes to work up to the goals you set for yourself.

CHAPTER FOUR

YOUR PLAN

Do good things happen in your life by chance? Some seem to think so; however, I know that when you think of things in a specific way, good things start to happen. This means that good things happen because of action and not because of chance. Our thoughts determine our future, and the key is to pay attention to your internal dialogue. Goals and "to do" lists are great, but they are often unachieved. The simple reason is that an "action plan" was never established. Have you ever thought about water? nothing can prevent water from flowing and streaming, that is called dynamic and mobility. if something blocks the water, it finds a way to go around so you should be like water. Research has consistently shown that people need to push themselves beyond their comfort zones to perform at their best. This is called embracing "optimal anxiety." It turns out that the more you are willing to challenge yourself, the more comfortable you will become with new experiences.

It can be terrifying to take risks, because we are generally not comfortable with the idea of failure. Most people are afraid of risk. However, people who do not take risks and push themselves are more likely to regret not doing so later in life. Getting out of your comfort zone occasionally can also help you develop the flexibility; you need to deal with life's unexpected roadblocks. When you live your life to the fullest, you take chances. You go after what you want. You make decisions that have consequences. And sometimes, these things do not go the way you had hoped. Embracing vulnerability, the possibility that things will go differently than we had planned, is crucial to experiencing life in a full, open, honest way.

Vulnerability helps you take actions in all areas of your life. If you are afraid of being open and honest with another person because you might get hurt, you will not be able to develop a truly intimate relationship. If you are afraid of taking a chance because it might not work out, you may miss opportunities.

Before taking any action, make sure your actions are aligned with your values, it is far more important than achieving success in the eyes of others. Your sense of self becomes fragile when it is dependent on external validation, instead be clear about your values and live by them because this is the strongest foundation of who you are. Do not be content to let your life just happen. Be active and present in it. Always consider what you can learn from whatever situation you encounter. This will help you avoid stressing over challenges and will keep you focused on moving forward, not looking back.

If you do this, it shapes your world continually and non-stop also it changes how you see it. Depending on what your internal dialogue says at key points in your life will determine not only how you feel about certain things but also what you believe about yourself and things around you and this will determine where the best is to spend your energy. your internal dialogue runs automatically if you let it however, if you pay attention to it, you can choose what you say to yourself. I am practicing every day what I say to myself and I have a lot of success so far although I am not perfect, but I see it affect in my life. When you know what, your goals are, you need to set a date to achieve those goals? If you do not set a date for achieving your goals, you never can measure your progress. Also, you should break down your goals into small levels, for example if you want to achieve certain level of money you need to break it down to quarter and then half of that money that you want to achieve. You need a strategy and an action plan to achieve your goals.

An action plan is a detailed plan outlining actions needed to reach one or more goals. It is an organizational strategy to identify necessary steps towards a goal. In some ways, an action plan is a "heroic" act: it helps us turn our dreams into a reality. It describes the way you will use strategies to meet your objectives. An action plan consists of several action steps. Each action step or change to be sought should include the following information

* What actions or changes will occur
* By when they will take place
* What resources (i.e., money, staff) are needed to carry out these changes

people often discouraged because of unrealistic or poorly planned goals. The smarter approach is to learn to embrace the process, like you are taking your eyes off the prize. You will not lose all the weight overnight, so your best option is to focus on making each day the best it can be. Chop up the big goal into a string of daily or weekly goals that are easier to accomplish. "A lot of research is showing us that we do much better when we focus on incremental change, or a little bit of improvement, "That is how you go from a couch potato to a marathoner. You temporarily ignore the fact you need to run 26 miles several months from now and focus only on running one mile today. And since that goal is much easier to achieve, you will feel a sense of accomplishment once it is complete. In turn, that creates the extra motivation you need to move onto a second and third run, and, ultimately, the race itself. The habit of having a daily action plan each day, will bring about amazing changes in your life, and in the lives of others.

What is a strategy?

A strategy is a way of describing how you are going to get thing done. A strategy is a way of describing how you are going to get things done. It is less specific than an action plan; instead, it tries to broadly answer the question, "How do we get there from here?" A good strategy will consider existing barriers and resources (people, money, power, materials, etc.). It will also stay with the overall vision and objectives of the initiative. Often, an initiative will use many different strategies--providing information, enhancing support, removing barriers, providing resources, etc.--to achieve its goals. Strategy is important because the resources available to achieve these goals are usually limited and you need strategy for mobilizing resources to execute the actions. A strategy describes how the ends goals will be achieved by the means (resources). This is generally tasked with determining strategy. A strategy should:

* Give overall direction, A strategy, such as enhancing experience and skill or increasing resources and opportunities, should point out the overall path.

* Fit resources and opportunities, A good strategy takes advantage of current resources and assets, such as people's willingness to act and community pride. It also embraces new opportunities such as an emerging public concern for neighborhood safety or parallel economic development efforts in the business community.

* Minimize resistance and barriers, when initiatives set out to accomplish important things, resistance (even opposition) is inevitable. However, strategies need not provide a reason for opponents to attack the initiative. Good strategies attract allies and deter opponents.

That is why I told you create your goals based on your values and categorize them, then plan. If you do not have enough money and you want to earn more money, nature of problem is different than when you want to lose weight. Guiding policy is also important, that is why you need strategy to deal with the problem after all of this you need action plan to execute the strategy.

Let me give you an example, I wanted to achieve some goals before, but I had to choose a strategy for achieving my goals, I needed some money which I did not have, so I had to choose between focusing on earning money then I could go after my goals or I could start my goals and Believe that money which I needed will be provided. They are different strategies with different mindset. You see my resources was limited and I had to use my resources in the best way possible. I had to use my money and my time wisely, I could not waste any of them. I am not saying it is easy because it needs a lot of efforts and discipline but it worth it.

Having discipline is hard but it saves you from pain of regret. You put yourself in difficult situation now to be comfortable in the future. For your action plan, you need to make a to do list based on your priorities and stick to it. Do you remember I talked about fear of change, combine that fear of risk with a lack of energy to work toward your goals, and a lack of confidence in our abilities, and it is no wonder we stay locked in our old habits and routines despite our unhappiness? To benefit from risk management action plans, you need to examine certain possibilities that could affect the process, such as observing any threats and correcting them. This is a major factor, as evaluating what happens during and after the project, will allow finding the positive and negative elements of each stage in the planning, providing you the ability to develop on the risks further.

You already wrote down your goals but if you did not prioritize them do it now! because you want to use the best of your ability and time, do not waste your time on things that are not important to you. Always evaluate your plan and measure your progress to see if there is any need for corrections. I have heard a lot of immigrants that they are not happy in their new country, but they do not do anything about it. They are afraid of change or they are lying. Going to a different country with different culture and most probably different language is scary, if you took risks before, just think about them and use them as an example for yourselves. It is like all area of your life, remember when you wanted to do something that scared you before, but it is normal to you now, for example driving a car at first is scary but you use to it when you do it repeatedly. It applies to everything, remember things that you have done before successfully, then you can do take risk again.

If you did everything that I said so far, congratulation, you are a halfway there to achieve your goal, because now you know what you want exactly and you have a system to reach your goal. Most of the people do not do that. A walk begins with one step and then another and another. No matter how long your journey seems, if you take enough steps in the right direction, you will eventually arrive at your desired destination…and truly have the life you have always wanted. It is important to have a group support or at least tell one of your family member or friends about your plans and let them ask you about actions that you took based on yours to do list. they make you accountable and motivate you to stick to the plan.

After one year take a rest and take a break for a while, do inventory and rearrange your action plan. Remember help others along the way. Do not put so much pressure on yourself, although it is working for some people but normally when you say I should do it, you do not like it and it create resistance but if you say I choose to do it, is better and you feel much better. Also, enjoy your journey and do not be hard on yourself because of mistakes. Break down your goals into smaller goals because they are easier to achieve. Do not be afraid of failure, even smallest step is a success. You should celebrate because of that.

When you create, your goals based on your interests, you are not obliged to do it because somebody told you to do that but because you love to achieve that goal, that is why I told you assess your values. After breaking down your steps and have an action plan, you need to stick to the plan, that is why I told you, tell to at least one person to make you accountable, but before that, you need to Change your internal dialogue. We talk to ourselves all the time in our minds. Even when we are not paying attention, these relentless mental debates deeply influence our feelings and ultimately, our behaviour and actions.

however, if you pay attention to it, you can choose what you say to yourself. The good news is that if you can become aware of these mental dialogues, notice the patterns, and turn them into productive statements, then you are empowered to overcome many unwelcome feelings and behaviour. Being an optimist or a pessimist boils down to the way you talk to yourself. Optimists believe that their own actions result in positive things happening, that they are responsible for their own happiness, and they can expect more good things to happen in the future. Optimists do not blame themselves when bad things happen. They view bad events as results of something outside of themselves. I did not blame myself for losing my job but saw it as a business decision that had nothing to do with me personally. Pessimists think the opposite way, however. They blame themselves for the bad things that happen in their lives and think that one mistake means more will inevitably come. Pessimists see positive events as flukes that are outside of their control—a lucky streak that probably will not happen again. When you are happy the muscles in your cheeks contract causing you to smile. Similarly, if you contract the muscles in your cheeks and you smile, this causes you to feel happy: they are both linked. This link is also true between what you think and what you feel. If you feel bad, it will be because you are thinking negative thoughts and if you feel good you will be thinking positive thoughts. These are generally unconscious (automatic); however, by paying attention to your thoughts you bring them into conscious (manual) awareness and can change them.

The action plan for your initiative should meet several criteria. Is the action plan:Develop an action plan composed of action steps that address all proposed changes. The plan should be complete, clear, and current. Additionally, the action plan should include information and ideas you have already gathered while brainstorming about your objectives and your strategies. What are the steps you must take to carry out your objectives while still fulfilling your vision and mission? although the plan might address general goals, you want to see them accomplished. the action steps will help you determine the specific actions you will take to help make your vision a reality. If your feelings are ever sometimes in control of you, this technique of listening will be of use to you and will give you an insight as to why this may be dominating your life. Once you have an awareness of what you are saying to yourself, you will find that thinking positively becomes much easier.

In the same way that the captain in the control room, powers the submarine, our thoughts power our feelings which subsequently leads onto controlling our future. On one hand if you are constantly thinking sad things which make you feel sad your behaviour will reflect this. You may keep your head down or stop talking to people and over time this will become an unhelpful habit and you may not want to go out of the house. As a knock-on effect, over time your personality will change, and your future might not turn out as you want it to. On the other hand, if you become aware of thoughts that are making you feel sad, decide to learn from them and change your thoughts; look at the positive side of things that will make you feel happy and empowered and your behaviour will start to reflect that. Over time you will install this positive thinking as a habit and will most likely start smiling at people and complementing them which will improve your personality and will ultimately determine your future.

Feeling positive will cause positive things to happen. It is the fundamental to the law of attraction. Wouldn't it be great if you could control how you handle certain situations? What if I told you that you could and that it is relatively simple to do? It is all about what you say to yourself in those certain situations that determines how you feel and how you move forward. The 80/20 rule is one of the most helpful concepts for life and time management. According to this principle: 20 percent of your activities will account for 80 percent of your results. It can change the way you set goals forever. people in society seemed to divide naturally into what called the "vital few," or the top 20 percent in terms of money and influence, and the "trivial many," or the bottom 80 percent.

If you have a list of ten items to accomplish, two of those items will turn out to be worth more than the other eight items put together. The sad fact is that most people procrastinate on the top 10 or 20 percent of items that are the most valuable and important, the "vital few," and busy themselves instead with the least important 80 percent, the "trivial many," that contribute truly little to their success Here is what you should do to effectively apply the 80/20 rule to goal setting and to your overall productivity. First, take a piece of paper and write down ten goals. Then ask yourself: If you could only accomplish one of the goals on that list today, which one goal would have the greatest positive impact on your life?

Then pick the second most important goal, you can choose five of them. after you complete this exercise, you will have determined the most important 20 percent of your goals that will help you more than anything else. You often see people who appear to be busy all day long but seem to accomplish little. This is almost always because they are busy working on tasks that are of low value while they are procrastinating on the one or two activities that could make a real difference to their companies and to their careers. The most valuable tasks you can do each day are often the hardest and most complex, but the payoff and rewards for completing them can be tremendous. Before you begin work, always ask yourself, "Is this task in the top 20 percent of my activities or in the bottom 80 percent?"

If you choose to start your day working on low-value tasks, you will soon develop the habit of always starting and working on low-value tasks. You are not by nature a contented person. It is our nature to want things to be different, to want them to be better. It is not our nature to be contented, and neither is yours. But if you are going to slow down your life, you should learn contentment. It is learned over time. He is saying life is not about things. I did not have anything before I was born. I am not going to have anything after I die. Yes, I need things, but they are not what life is about, so I will just be content with what I have got.

Let me explain what contentment is not. Contentment is not abandoning your ambition. You ought to have ambition. You ought to make the most of what God has given you. God says it is good to have godly ambition. Contentment does not mean you do not have any goals, dreams, or plans for your life.

Contentment means this: You do not need more to be happy. You are happy right now with what you have been given. Happiness is a choice. You are as happy as you choose to be! You cannot blame unhappiness on your circumstances. If you are not happy with your circumstances, you have a choice accept your situation, appreciate what you have and change it or complain and do not do anything, then you are not going to be happy with different situation. There will always be something wrong. We live on a broken planet, and nothing is perfect. God wants you to learn to be happy despite difficult situations by trusting that he will give you exactly what you need when you need it. Since learning contentment is a process, what is one step you can take today to practice gratitude?

Chapter Five

Action Plan

I have talked enough about making a list of what you want and how to arrange them according to importance and your values, now we get to the important part which is "action plan". you know what you want, now is the time to set a date for them, and as I suggested brock them into small steps to be more achievable. For example, if you want to lose 50 pounds in 5 month you set your goal as lose ten pound in the next month and after achieving that goal you set another goal lose 10 pounds again in next month in this way you are motivated and you do not be discouraged by how far you should go to reach your goal.

Gratitude is not just a feeling; it is a way of life that requires active practice. Research shows that practicing gratitude makes you feel healthier, happier, and more positive. Gratitude can help you overcome past trauma and strengthen your relationships with others. Recognize daily things you are grateful for. Let your family, friends, and other significant ones know how grateful you are to have them. Share and express love while you can. Your life will feel more fulfilling when you actively practice being grateful. Humans have a bad tendency to focus on the negative aspects of life and ignore all the beauty and positivity around us. Take the time to acknowledge and savor the small moments of beauty in your everyday life. Think about what this experience means to you. Be mindful of the happiness it is bringing to your life in that moment. Writing these experiences down can be helpful. Even small things, such as an unexpected text from a friend or a beautiful sunny morning, can fill us with gratitude if we let them.

Share your gratitude with others. You are more likely to "store" positive things in your memory if you share them with other people. If you see a gorgeous flower while you are riding the bus, text a friend to let her know about it. If your partner did the dishes as a surprise for you, tell him how much you appreciate it. Sharing your gratitude can also help others feel positive and inclined to look for ways to be grateful in their lives.

It is not enough to make them into small piece, but you should know what your plan is to achieve them precisely, every day that you wake up you should know what steps you should take to be closer to your goals. I use google calendar to organize my daily activity, I set out my goal and put a period for that activity, one of my goals is to be more flexible in my body and I want to have more endurance, so my action plan is exercise 5 days a week and I set a period for that. for me exercise in the morning is better so I exercise 5 days in a week around 8 am.

Identifying action steps from your action plan is essential for achieving your goals. Determining action steps helps you find practical ways to reach your objectives and focus on the details necessary to succeed. This section provides a guide for developing action steps to increase the efficiency.

WHAT IS AN ACTION STEP?

An action step refers to the specific efforts that are made to reach the goals you set. Action steps are the exact details of your action plan. They should be concrete and comprehensive, and each action step should explain:

- What will occur
- How much, or to what extent, these actions will occur
- When these actions will take place, and for how long
- What resources (such as money) are needed to carry out the proposed actions

WHY SHOULD YOU IDENTIFY ACTION STEPS?

Anticipating the future makes us feel in control, right? That is the major reason identifying action steps is important. You can get prepared for what your next step should be. Other reasons are:

- ➤ To concentrate on the details that must occur to succeed in your mission
- ➤ To decide on workable ways to reach your goals
- ➤ To save time, energy, and resources overall: a well-structured, thought -out action plan will make things much easier for you

WHEN SHOULD YOU DETERMINE ACTION STEPS?

You should determine your action steps after you have decided what changes you want to occur. You probably do this anyway, at least on a casual level; you decide what changes you want to see occur, and then you decide how to go about making them. These "how's" are your action steps.

HOW DO YOU IDENTIFY ACTION STEPS?

Brainstorm different, specific ways that your strengths can be used to carry out the changes that you have decided upon.
Consider the possible barriers to implementing your proposed changes, and possible ways to remove these barriers. Some questions you might ask yourselves include:
- Do I have enough money to carry out my action steps?
- Do I have enough time to carry out these changes?
- Are these action steps can get people excited about?
- What kind of opposition can I expect if I put my plan into effect? Are there ways to get around it"

Use the SCHEMES* mnemonic to check that your plan is comprehensive. SCHEMES stand for:

Space.
Cash.
Helpers/People.
Equipment.
Materials.
Expertise.

Do you have space needed for your actions or goals, space has two meaning one of them is actual location to do your activity, for example maybe you need a quiet place for writing or study. The other meaning of space is boundaries, do you allow yourself to make a mistake or do you allow other people to make a mistake. When you plan, there is always set back, discouragement and failure, do not give up on your plan, be persistent, after every failure, regroup, stand tall and start again.
- Do you have enough cash to execute your plan, if not you should have a plan to get that money?
- Do you have people to help you, they might be your friend, mentor and coach or employee?
- Do you have equipment that you need to reach your goal?
- Do you have materials you need?

- Do you have expertise you need?

Have a journal and write down lessons that you are learning because we often forget what we learned before. Look for opportunity in every situation to learn something, for example when you are in traffic jam, you can practice patience.

We all have those days when we work too hard on the wrong things, but we should make sure that those days do not turn into weeks or months and certainly not years. An audit will leave you with the clarity and space you need to "do it" at the ultimate level.

Here are the three steps to conducting a Life Audit:

1. **Mission**

Quality life advice will not be helpful to you if you do not know your personal mission. What is your 'why'? What is the vision for your life? If you are not clear on the answers to these questions, then it will be hard for you to set the direction of your audit. It is up to you to carve your life's direction and it is a power move to dig deep and put your goals on paper. A personal mission statement will help you articulate your values, beliefs, determine your personal definition of success, how you contribute value to the world, and help you show others the current purpose of your life. As you design this guide look up the personal mission statements of other professionals for a template or consult your favorite companies for strong examples.

2. **Flare**

What is currently on your plate? Make a master list of everything in your life that is taking up time. Full-time jobs, relationships, community involvements, social media accounts, and whatever else that might be taking up space in your life. After you have completed this task you will take this list along with your mission statement and seek points of agreement between the two. Where there's agreement, there exists an opportunity to clean up some space on your plate of life. Questions to consider:

- How is this helping me achieve my mission?
- Do I enjoy it? Some things you might just want to keep around because it is fun. Fun is allowed!
- What am I gaining by having this on my plate? Could you achieve the same gains another way?
- What would I lose by taking this off my plate? Do those things play a large role in me achieving my mission?
- Is this taking other resources from me that could be useful in helping me live out my mission? Are you finding it hard to find time to sit down and write your book, but you are giving 3 hours of your week to something you feel "meh" about? It could be good to push this stuff off your plate now in order to fulfill the larger mission.
- If I were not already involved with this, would I sign up for it now? If the

answer is 'no' then that is an easy thing to cross off your list.

- Is this helping me to fulfill the basic needs of life? For instance, my workout costs are expensive, but my health is critically important. I can always research cheaper options, but I shouldn't give up fitness altogether.

Go through your list and be strong. Always think back to your mission. If you need a little guidance, try the stoplight method:

RED: STOP! These are things that you must say no to them right now.

YELLOW: Slow Down! You can still be involved but maybe at a different level. This is a commitment that you need to redesign.

GREEN: GO! Mission agreement and a life must-have.

Collect what you have left on your list. If your new plate seems more manageable and will help you lead to your personal definition of success, then you have had a successful audit. If not, then rinse and repeat. You might find some gaps during your audit and this could lead to adding new opportunities to your plate but be sure that you have the capacity to handle adding things to your plate. Exchanges will likely have to happen between a new and existing opportunity.

Having a personal mission statement allows you to flare and focus with purpose. As new opportunities come your way you can run them through your mission filter. Set up a regular time to engage in a Life Audit. Re-examine and rework your mission as needed, flare and put everything in front of you and then focus to commit to those things that will help you achieve success.

After you have done all of this, you need to consider few things:

1-Do not be held back by what happened yesterday, the day before, the week before, the year before, and so on.

2-Maybe you cannot achieve your goals easily, do not try shortcuts, stay true to yourself, it is better to be original version of yourself.

3-Stop complaining about your problems and work on them instead.

4-Stop waiting for others around you to do something and act yourself instead.

5-Let go of things that you cannot control.

6-Be committed to your growth. In the Map of Consciousness, there are 17 levels of consciousness – from Shame to Enlightenment. The higher level of consciousness you are in, the richer your life experience. Achieving higher consciousness comes from your commitment to growth.

7-Do not do things for the sake of doing them. Always evaluate what you are doing and only do it if there is meaning behind them. Do not be afraid to quit the things that do not serve your path.

8-Be the absolute best in what you do. Go for the #1 position in what you do. If you want to spend your time doing something, you might as well be the best in it. Strive for the best – you do not deserve anything lesser than that.

9-Behave as your ideal self-will. All of us have an ideal vision of who we want to be. How is your ideal self like? How can you start to be that ideal self now?

10-Blind spots (defined in the context of personal development) refer to the aspects of ourselves we are not fully conscious of. This can refer to a broad spectrum of different things – our traits, values, actions, habits, feelings, thoughts, etc. This reason is usually beyond our immediate observation – we can only identify them when we probe deeper. Blind spots are not as immediately observable to us compared to people around us, such as friends who have known us for a while or someone who is trained to identify them, like a life coach.

Why is it important to know your blind spots? Because it is a necessary part of your personal growth. Blind spots are things you are unaware of. Identifying our blind spots and understanding them heightens our level of self-awareness. When we develop a greater self-awareness, it puts us in greater alignment with our higher selves and who we are meant to be. The net result is a speedier progression toward achieving your own level of greatness. Getting a personal coach is an excellent way to uncover your own blind spots so that you can become better. When you are oblivious to something, there is a high likelihood that:

(1) you have never worked on it before, which leaves an opportunity for improvement.

(2) it is acting as an invisible boundary that limits your experience in your life.

When you uncover your blind spots and actively work on them, you start becoming more conscious as an individual, of your strengths and opportunity areas, the boundaries you operate within. If you do not uncover these blind spots, you will never be able to work on them, simply because you are not aware of their existence.

11-Help others live their best lives. There is no better way to grow than to help others grow. Ultimately, the world is one. We are all in this together.

12-Give more value than you receive. There is so much unspeakable joy that comes from giving. And when you keep giving, you will find that you receive a lot more in return, in spades.

13-The only person you can change is yourself. Stop expecting others to behave in a certain way. Rather than demand that others around you change, focus on changing yourself. You will be happier and live a more fulfilling life this way.

14-Embrace and express gratitude: be grateful and let people know of your gratitude toward them.

15-Challenge your fears. All of us have fears. Fear of uncertainty, fear of public speaking, fear of risk... All our fears keep us in the same position and prevent us from growing. Rather than avoid your fears, recognize they

are the compass for growth. Address and overcome them.
16-Remember that everything happens in your life is for your own benefit.
17-Be humble as you go forward
18-When we keep an open mind to new ideas and different ways of thinking we broaden our minds to see how things work from a new perspective. We all think and see things differently and it is from these differences that we can receive some of our greatest lessons and growth. Allow yourself to embrace those new ways of thinking and to learn something from every single person that you meet.

19-Enjoy the little things in life. There are little pleasures of life you can celebrate each day. The little things could be as simple as you are getting good nights' sleep, the smell of coffee in a coffee shop, a hug from a friend, the smell of rain on the horizon, the sparkle of a rainbow in the sky, the refreshment of ice-cold water, or the first taste of a glass of wine. They may be small, but they should always be appreciated, as it is the little things that really make up life.
20-Contribute to the world, give back and be generous with your time. Words, love, ideas, and money. Let the world and the people around you feed off your positivity and generosity. A smile is contagious and so is the power of being and staying positive.
21-Don't aim for perfection, nobody is perfect.
22-Remember take responsibility for your actions and do not blame anybody
23-Everything happens for your own good, do not ask why me?
24-Everybody who tries anything worthwhile fails at some point or the other. Failure does not mean we are broken. It simply means we are courageous to dare! Easier said than done, but I am trying.
25-Anger will eat at you from the inside. Learn how to make peace with those who have wronged you. This is not about letting the other person off the hook; it is about alleviating the pain that resonates within you. Keep in mind that he who angers you, controls you.
26-Too many people live their lives with the thought that they will be millionaires. While this can be a realistic goal for some, it is not something that can be achieved without hard work and dedication. Stop letting money be your sole motivator; find a career you are passionate about and immerse yourself in it completely.
The person I have become today and the person I was in the past is quite different, and it was not through luck or accident. It was through conscious desire and work
•Ignore the haters. No matter what you decide to do with your life, there will always be someone around to point out the many ways you will fail. Know that every winner loses, but not every loser wins. Successful people

do not start out successful. What makes them successful is that they keep pushing through failure.

- Do not compromise your values. If something does not feel right, do not do it. Do not compromise on your internal code of ethics. Life does not work like a movie. It is filled with gray areas. Trust your instincts. Do whatever you want so long as you can look yourself in the mirror.
- Do charitable acts for others. Every day, you will see someone who could use help. It is easy to look at a homeless person on the street and think, "I wish I could help him." What will happen if you do? If you gave $1 to that homeless person every day, you would be out $365 a year if you worked every day. It does not take much.
- Keep your mind open. Just because you are right about something does not mean there are no other ways to look at it. Listening to ideas you do not agree with or understand keeps your brain active and healthy.

One of the best things in life is you are free to take part in the things which you believe is true and meaningful. Different people in this world fight for different things in their life. Some fight for the animals and give them a lot of love unconditionally, some protect the future generation ensuring they have sufficient and up to standard living condition, some save the earth and call for a greener and cleaner place to stay, and some provide urgent medical care in countries to victims of war and disaster regardless of race, religion, or politics. Ask yourself what you genuinely believe in and what you think it is worth to strive for in your life. Join related non-profit organization and start acting. You can enrich your life while doing all the meaningful right things.

Living life to the fullest means continually reaching out for newer, richer, deeper, life-changing experiences. It means using those experiences as a means for personal growth and pushing the boundaries of yourself mentally, spirituality, and intellectually for the betterment of yourself and the world at large.

The key to living life to the fullest is opening your mind and stretching beyond your comfort zone. Because if you are not being challenged or intentionally pushing yourself beyond the realm of things that are familiar to you, then the experiences you are having are no longer validated. by your values and do things in life that resonate with you. As an entrepreneur, you are often so consumed with your venture that you forget to take a step back and put everything into perspective. But a death in my family recently forced me to do this, making me reflect on how I hope to live life to the fullest.

Living a life of authenticity. Live by your values and do things in life that resonate with your core – regardless of what others think. Despite years of disapproval, I never looked back, and knew I made the right decision.

Not letting fear hold you back. As a beginner surfer, this is one of the things I often struggle with out on the water. There is no scarier feeling than being held under by a wave, frantically trying to find your way back to the surface. But I know if I do not let go of that fear, I will never have the chance to improve my skills, or to catch the best waves.

Similarly, I try to not let fear hold me back in other aspects of my life. Starting a business and moving to India for four years to launch it was one of the scariest things I have ever done. But by focusing on my mission, rather than being overwhelmed by possibility of failure, I could forge ahead. You never want to miss an amazing opportunity because you were too scared to give it a try. Know in the face of failure, you can simply try again.

Defining yourself by your values, not by external validation. It is so easy to let your sense of self-worth be defined by what others think about you, or by achieving certain goals, recognitions, or accolades. As an entrepreneur, you are constantly moving from one goal to the next, always trying to achieve the next milestone: that flashy award, quarterly revenue goal, or prestigious speaking opportunity.

Conclusion

Congratulations! You finished reading this, I hope you read it again and again and apply it in your life. To go somewhere, you need to know your present location, that is why I suggested assessing your situation first, also I give you advice that which area you should focus to assess your situation, but it is your choice you can ignore some of them or add a few. Based on my experience those are important to have a balanced life and like everything else in life you need to have a foundation and build a balanced structure on top of that foundation. In order to do that you need knowledge and application of that knowledge in your life. For example, everyone knows smoking cigarette is dangerous even it is written in the box, but if you do not pay any attention to it there is no use! And honesty is particularly important to assess your situation because most of the people are in denial position. You cannot change anything if you are not aware that it needs to be changed.

after assessing your situation, you need to know, what do you want and why do you want it? In every area, you have some needs, and it might be different depend on your age and your belief system, but you should be certain that it is your need and not anybody else opinion or you want it because of wrong reasons. For example, you want something because you want to impress others which is wrong, there is a difference between what you want and what you need. Next step is , take action and go forward , you already know what you want, then you need a map and action plan to go there , you need to know how you can get there, that is why I showed you how you can make an action plan and go forward , I reminded you there will be obstacles, ups and down but if you know why do you want that things nothing can stop you , don't look back always , always look ahead and what do you want to achieve , but don't focus on what you want , enjoy the journey and you will get there if you don't exit .

from the way that is right way to achieve your goals. You should remember some point along the way:

1- be positive all the time, to apply this to your life you need to listen to motivational messages every day, all of us came across negative thoughts and disappointment but you need to shift your mind at least once a day to have hope and encouragement all the time.

2- help others along the way, it is good to focus on your goals and I recommend it but if you want to go far you need to help others to achieve their goals, in this way you get help in times of needs and satisfaction also it helps to forget your problems.

3- do not try to be perfect, no one and no action can be perfect, do not stress yourself by being perfectionist.

4- do not let your fear or your circumstances control you, dare to change yourself and accept your fear and deal with that fear, also do not let anybody or any situation dictate you what you should do.

5- there is no short cut, do not compromise your values to achieve your goals, be authentic and do not wear a mask.

6- be original, do not try to copy anybody, you are unique, and you can do something that nobody can do it.

7- set your boundaries, it is good to help others and make them happy and provide their needs, but you cannot please everybody, sometimes you need to say no.

8- never stock in a situation, you always can do better, be better and reach further goals.

Other books from this author

church structure
organizational leadership

divinity of
Jesus Christ

Life in the forks

true gospel series
God's election
Christian behaviors
Philosophy of humanity
Grace
Prayer

ABOUT THE AUTHOR

Dr. Mohsen is a distinguished speaker and author with Big vision, his specialty is spiritual matters. he reached so many lost souls and helped lives get started and changed. after a long time, suffering from difficulties, he dedicated himself to help others and teach the truth about God and Christianity. he is founder of two ministry which are foundations of life and speakup production which are in service to the people who are eager to learn and grow. he is a strong believer of hands-on training and simplicity, that is why he always find a way to teach others about integrity and truth in a simple form. he holds Doctorates Degree in organizational leadership and D. Min with honors in Ministry.

CPSIA information can be obtained
at www.ICGtesting.com
Printed in the USA
LVHW080247240822
726749LV00015B/1162